#B2B STRATEGIC PRICING tweet Book01

Game-Changing Pricing Strategies
for Manufacturing and Service Companies

By Bob Bonacorsi

An Actionable Business Journal

E-mail: info@thinkaha.com
20660 Stevens Creek Blvd., Suite 210
Cupertino, CA 95014

Copyright © 2014 Bob Bonacorsi

All rights reserved. No part of this book shall be reproduced, stored in a retrieval system, or transmitted by any means electronic, mechanical, photocopying, recording, or otherwise without written permission from the publisher.

Published by THiNKaha®
20660 Stevens Creek Blvd., Suite 210, Cupertino, CA 95014
http://thinkaha.com

First Printing: April 2014
Paperback ISBN: 978-1-61699-126-5 (1-61699-126-7)
eBook ISBN: 978-1-61699-127-2 (1-61699-127-5)
Place of Publication: Silicon Valley, California, USA
Paperback Library of Congress Number: 2013947810

Trademarks

All terms mentioned in this book that are known to be trademarks or service marks have been appropriately capitalized. Neither THiNKaha, nor any of its imprints, can attest to the accuracy of this information. Use of a term in this book should not be regarded as affecting the validity of any trademark or service mark.

Warning and Disclaimer

Every effort has been made to make this book as complete and as accurate as possible. The information provided is on an "as is" basis. The author(s), publisher, and their agents assume no responsibility for errors or omissions. Nor do they assume liability or responsibility to any person or entity with respect to any loss or damages arising from the use of information contained herein.

Advance Praise

"*#B2B STRATEGIC PRICING tweet* is a good high-level view of what is involved in pricing correctly for both products and services. It focuses on concepts and would be great for a new marketing employee to read. This is not a 'how-to' book, but rather a book that focuses on the questions of 'what and why,' which are often more important. If the principles in the book are followed it can result in a great ROI, and strategies that don't leave any money on the table."

David Coleman, Founder & Senior Analyst, Collaborative Strategies, Inc. (http://www.collaborativeshift.com)

"Strategic pricing: overlooked and not in the spotlight. For those very reasons an important read for business executives and directors."

Allan Grafman, CEO, All Media Ventures

"Much of pricing in the corporate world is done by gut feel and committee, leaving massive money on the table. *#B2B STRATEGIC PRICING tweet* is a great read, with immediately actionable knowledge to dramatically increase your company's profits."

Brian Lawley, CEO & Founder, 280 Group LLC

"Pricing is confounding for companies, especially manufacturers who are often consumed with the day-to-day rigor of producing and distributing a product. Bob Bonacorsi's experience and training has taught him that many small and mid-size companies need a system and a process for pricing. Bob has filled that need. With a keen focus on value through the eyes of the customer, Bob will help you build a strategy based on value that increases margins. It's simply brilliant! He'll help you leapfrog your competition as they follow outdated, product-oriented, and low-margin practices."

Jay R. McKeever, Director of Worldwide Marketing, Cincom Systems, Inc.

"By starting with strategic pricing and providing useful guidelines for new products, change management, and continuous improvement, Bob Bonacorsi's book is filled with bite-sized words of wisdom that make for a great handbook for those looking to improve pricing performance. This is a great tool that can help companies improve margins and profitability."

Kevin M. Mitchell, President, The Professional Pricing Society, Inc., Atlanta, GA

"In #B2B STRATEGIC PRICING tweet, Bob Bonacorsi offers great insight and pointers to product managers, sales teams, and operating executives. He succinctly articulates the key principles in optimizing value between an organization and its customers. In doing so, he shows how a proactive pricing strategy is a win-win strategy, which not only improves customer loyalty, but also minimizes 'leakage' and thus maximizes long-term corporate profits."

Rudy Mui, Chief Operating Officer, Aqua Metrology Systems

"My kind of book: short, pithy, focused, concentrated, extremely useful. Written by someone who has been there."

Mike Prevou, Author, #SUCCESSFUL CORPORATE LEARNING tweet Book05: Everything You Need to Know about Knowledge Management in Practice in 140 Characters or Less

"Strategic pricing is something of value for all members of your team because it is smart to know how to price your products and services. Most importantly, it is about the customer and their experience in working with your organization. Bob will show you not only how to avoid catastrophic pricing decisions but how to use strategic pricing to enhance customer relations and the customer experience with your company."

Patrick Reilly, President, Resources In Action, Inc.

"In today's competitive marketplace and constant state of change, you cannot underestimate the importance of strategic pricing. Bob Bonacorsi provides quick-hit insight and education about this often overlooked lever you have to add value to any business."

Sal Silvester, Author, *Ignite! The 4 Essential Rules for Emerging Leaders*

"Bob has written a concise, important book about strategic pricing. A game-changing topic that is not well understood."

Bob Wright, Managing Partner, Firebrick Consulting

Acknowledgments

First, I would like to thank my wife, Linda, for providing both moral support and the time required for me to write this book. It would have been much more difficult without her full cooperation. I thank Mitchell Levy for providing me with the inspiration to write about this topic for which we share a strong mutual interest. Without his influence, I may never have even gotten started. I also want to thank my editor, Diane Vo, for educating me, a first-time author, on the process of writing clearly and staying focused on the task at hand.

Why I Wrote This Book

Strategic pricing is a game-changing process for business-to-business pricing in today's highly competitive global markets. While it is practiced by many of the world's leading corporations, it is not well understood by the majority of small- to medium-sized businesses. It has a significant, positive impact on the profitability of companies that have employed it effectively. It is not unusual for a company to increase its bottom line by two to three points or more within the first two years after implementation. After all, what company doesn't want to add another three hundred thousand dollars to the bottom line for every ten million dollars in sales? And the real win is that these companies are also growing their businesses and improving customer satisfaction at the same time.

Every year that I spent as a marketing manager developing and integrating this process further into our organization and seeing the benefits, I became a bigger proponent of strategic pricing. I also became more certain that all manufacturing and service companies with annual sales of twenty million dollars or more (or start-ups that strive to achieve over twenty million dollars) should absolutely integrate strategic pricing into their business processes. The earlier a new company incorporates this process, the easier it is to implement and have the process become ingrained in the company culture.

Seeking further and more diverse knowledge in this field, I became a member of the Professional Pricing Society™ and began additional training to augment my six years of in-house training and practice. In 2012 I achieved their recognition as a Certified Pricing Professional™.

During the course of my training, I was unable to find a book that provided a concise introduction and overview of business-to-business strategic pricing for senior managers and executives. As a result, I decided to write this book to fill that need.

As a manager or executive, this book will enable you to:
- Gain a basic understanding of strategic pricing and how it will benefit your company
- Understand how strategic pricing integrates into your business processes

- Learn how best-practice pricing strategies differ for various market segments and buyers
- Appreciate the critical nature of pricing new products and services correctly at launch
- Discover how companies can implement price changes and increase customer satisfaction
- Measure pricing-process performance and achieve continuous improvement

Bob Bonacorsi
bbonacorsi@profitsmartsolutions.com

How to Read a THiNKaha® Book
A Note from the Publisher

The THiNKaha series is the CliffsNotes of the 21st century. The value of these books is that they are contextual in nature. Although the actual words won't change, their meaning will change every time you read one as your context will change. Experience your own "aha!" moments ("ahas") with a THiNKaha book; ahas are looked at as "actionable" moments—think of a specific project you're working on, an event, a sales deal, a personal issue, etc. and see how the ahas in this book can inspire your own ahas, something that you can specifically act on. Here's how to read one of these books and have it work for you.

1. Read a THiNKaha book (these slim and handy books should only take about 15–20 minutes of your time!) and write down one to three actionable items you thought of while reading it. Each journal-style THiNKaha book is equipped with space for you to write down your notes and thoughts underneath each aha.
2. Mark your calendar to re-read this book again in 30 days.
3. Repeat step #1 and write down one to three more ahas that grab you this time. I guarantee that they will be different than the first time. BTW: this is also a great time to reflect on the actions taken from the last set of ahas you wrote down.

After reading a THiNKaha book, writing down your ahas, re-reading it, and writing down more ahas, you'll begin to see how these books contextually apply to you. THiNKaha books advocate for continuous, lifelong learning. They will help you transform your ahas into actionable items with tangible results until you no longer have to say "aha!" to these moments—they'll become part of your daily practice as you continue to grow and learn.

As Thought Leader Architect & CEO of THiNKaha, I definitely practice what I preach. I read *#POSITIVITY at WORK tweet*, *#MANAGING YOUR VIRTUAL BOSS tweet*, and one new book once a month and take away two to three different action items from each of them every time. Please e-mail me your ahas today!

Mitchell Levy
publisher@thinkaha.com

Contents

Section I
Strategic Pricing: What Is It and
Why Is It So Important?   15

Section II
Pricing Strategies   33

Section III
Pricing New Products and Services   51

Section IV
Strategic Pricing Goals and Metrics   65

Section V
Implementing a Strategic Pricing
Process for Your Business   77

Section VI
Implementing Price Changes   95

Section VII
Continuous Improvement   109

Appendix: Pricing Analytics   121

About the Author   125

Section I: What Is It and Why Is It So Important?

Section I
What Is It and Why Is It So Important?

Strategic pricing synthesizes information from disparate functional areas, such as finance, accounting, marketing, and sales, to produce optimal pricing decisions. For example, while marketing managers have the responsibility to *anticipate* the market value created using customer and competitive data, the sales department is ultimately responsible for *communicating* this value to the customer. These departments must work with each other as well, and then the finance department can set appropriate financial objectives based on incremental profitability.

Pricing is both an art and a science. Pricers must ground their work in quantitative approaches while also employing sound judgment in dealing with the more ambiguous qualitative issues that are common in pricing problems. Successful pricing strategies should always follow the three guiding principles of strategic pricing by being *value-based*, *proactive*, and *profit driven*.[1]

There are several reasons why implementation of strategic pricing strategies is so important in today's business environment:

- Proliferation of product substitutes
- Increased competition
- Advances in technology
- Other environmental factors that necessitate smarter, faster, and more frequent pricing alternatives

Perhaps most importantly, price has more impact than other key profit drivers, such as cost reduction and volume increases. The chart on the next page (Figure 1) illustrates the relative impact of different profit drivers.

---

[1]. Thomas T. Nagle and John E. Hogan, PhD, *The Strategy and Tactics of Pricing: A Guide to Growing More Profitably*, 4th edition (Upper Saddle River, NJ: Pearson/Prentice Hall, 2006).

Section I: What Is It and Why Is It So Important?

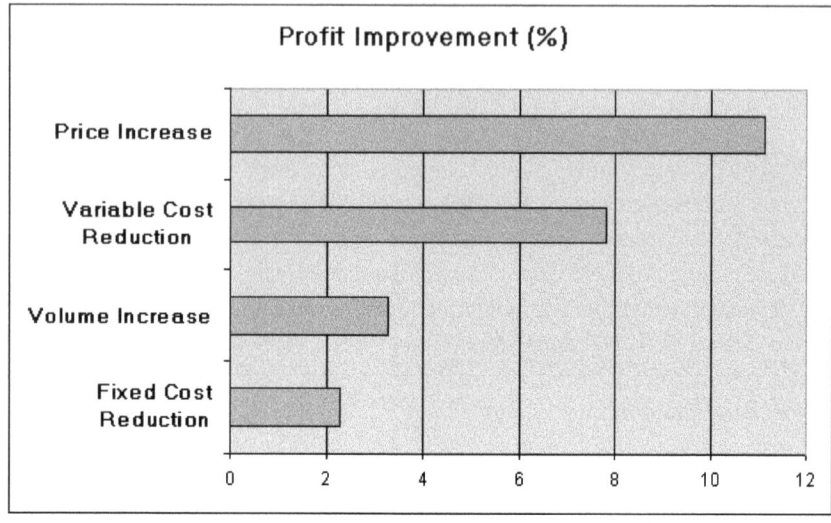

Figure 1: profit impact of a 1% change in each profit element[2]

---

2. Jerry Bernstein, "Managing Limited Resources to Improve Profitability," *The Journal of Professional Pricing*, November 3, 2006.

1

Pricing strategy is anchored in the company vision as it represents the perceived economic value of the firm's products to its customers.[3]

---

3. Stephan A. Butscher and Mark Billige, "Core Pricing Skills" (online pricing course provided by Professional Pricing Society), *Professional Pricing Society*, June 2009.

2

To surpass the limitations of traditional pricing structures, companies should adopt strategic pricing.

3

Strategic pricing is a proactive approach to pricing that can transform your company into a pricing leader rather than a follower.

4

Constructive pricing behavior and initiatives typically increase contribution margins by up to 50% and lifts gross margins 10%-15%.[4]

---

[4]. Jeffrey Johnson, "How to Organize the Pricing Discipline," *The Pricing Advisor* (monthly newsletter published by Professional Pricing Society), April 2006, http://members.pricingsociety.com/articles/April_2006.pdf.

5

Pricing is the only element of the 4 P's of marketing (product, pricing, placement, promotion) that generates revenue.

___

6

Companies typically spend fewer resources on their pricing processes than on cost reduction processes, even though pricing has more impact.

7

Cost-based pricing is the more commonly practiced strategy but value-based pricing results in more optimum (and more profitable) pricing.

_____
_____
_____

8

Value pricing starts with the customer and ends with the product. Cost-based pricing starts with the product and ends with the customer.

9

Compared to value pricing, cost-plus pricing will almost always result in either reduced sales volume or reduced profits.[5]

---

5. Nagle and Hogan, *The Strategy and Tactics of Pricing*.

10

For pricing to become a core competency, pricers must incorporate the 5 C's of value: create, comprehend, communicate, convince, capture.

11

Some companies base their prices on the marketplace. This approach tends to commoditize their products and significantly reduces margins.

12

When value is absent from the customer relationship, price usually becomes the primary factor in the customer's buying decision.

13

Strategic pricing increases customer satisfaction through ongoing dialogue with customers to provide their perception of product value.

14

A fully implemented strategic pricing process typically delivers an additional 3 points (& potentially up to 10 points) to pre-tax earnings.

15

Companies suffer significant "price leakage" that results from too many people with pricing authority and too few pricing control systems.

16

Pricing is like any other company process. If too many people touch it and no one owns it, it won't be aligned with overall business goals.

17

Strategic pricing brings a precise set of KPIs to measure, track, and optimize pricing, which doesn't exist in many organizations.

18

Companies that fail to segment their customers are unable to prioritize their sales and marketing efforts to optimize segment profits.

19

Companies that hold their prices at the same level for too long are eventually forced to implement a large increase, prompting customer ire.

20

Without strategic pricing, managers are often required to make pricing decisions based on incomplete/inaccurate information ("gut feel").

21

Pricers who lack an understanding of the basic price/volume/profit tradeoff often set price levels that are either too high or too low.

22

When sales incentives are not aligned with profitability goals, sales teams often spend the most time with the least profitable customers.

23

Today's leading companies are integrating pricing strategies into their organizational structure to optimize growth and profitability.

24

A properly implemented strategic pricing process provides a framework for managing both long-term strategies and daily pricing decisions.

_____

_____

_____

Section II: Pricing Strategies

Section II
Pricing Strategies

Pricing strategy is technically defined as "managing customers' expectations to induce them to pay for the value they receive. Pricing strategy is the coordination of multiple activities to achieve a common objective: profitable prices."[6]

Different customer, market, and product segments, in addition to products versus services, may each require unique strategies in order to optimize prices and, therefore, profitability. Ideal pricing strategies are also somewhat adaptive to market changes. Developing good pricing strategies is challenging but, when properly developed and executed, they often result in the most rapid path to significant profit enhancement.

In this section, we'll consider various strategies that can be used for the pricing of physical products depending upon key internal and external elements, such as the uniqueness and value of the product, price/volume elasticity, and different types of customer behavior.

We will discuss the differences between physical products and services and how these differences often provide increased flexibility in pricing strategies for services.

We will also identify types of buyers and how their focus and behaviors differ.

---

6. George Cressman and Thom Nagle, "Don't Just Set Prices, Manage Them," *The Pricing Advisor*, January 2003.

Section II: Pricing Strategies

25

To be effective, pricing strategies and sales and marketing strategies must be aligned with the overall business strategies of a company.

___

26

Proactive pricing implies taking a leadership position in pricing, be it for a market segment or an industry.

___

27

There are 3 proactive strategies that can be utilized depending on business goals: skim pricing, penetration pricing, and value pricing.

28

Skim prices are designed to capture high margins at the expense of volume and tend to be most effective in niche markets.

29

A variation of skim pricing is sequential skimming, which adjusts to capture different levels of price-sensitive niche buyers.

30

Penetration pricing is based on pricing aggressively to increase market share, which can be appropriate when costs and demand are elastic.

Section II: Pricing Strategies

31

Value pricing is designed to provide the product at a price that accurately reflects its market value relative to competitive products.

32

Value pricing is most effective when customer communication and relationships have been developed to create a mutual understanding of value.

33

A seller may elect to use skim, penetration, and/or value pricing strategies based upon the market and customer segments involved.

Section II: Pricing Strategies

34

While pricing should not be based on cost, cost does have a role to play, particularly when cost/volume elasticity is significant.

35

The cost/volume relationship is often elastic for physical products and inelastic for services, which increases service-pricing flexibility.

36

Services are different from products that are manufactured, grown, mined, or processed.[7]

---

7. Boris A. Simkovich, "The Sophisticated Pricing of Services," *The Journal of Professional Pricing*.

37

Services are non-tangible, non-transferable, and non-storable. They also frequently benefit from the existence of networks.[8]

38

Service prices are often based on soft attributes, are time-customized, or they can have fixed and variable components.

---

8. Ibid.

39

The top service sellers and top service sales managers rank price last in importance. Quality of service is much more influential.[9]

---

9. Alfred P. Hahn, "The Fundamentals of Services Pricing" (online pricing course provided by Professional Pricing Society), *Professional Pricing Society*, 2010.

Section II: Pricing Strategies

40

A strategy to be avoided: pricing services as a percent of the product price or a percent of the market leader's service price.

41

When developing a pricing strategy, it is necessary to understand that there are some distinctly different buyer behaviors.

42

Price buyers focus on purchasing "commodities" at the lowest price and are unlikely to pay for additional value.[10]

---

10. Dr. Reed K. Holden, "Getting Out of the Professional Services Commodity Trap," *The Journal of Professional Pricing* 14, no. 2 (2005).

43

Value buyers are willing to pay for more value if it is relevant to their business operations.[11]

44

Relationship buyers rely on trusted advisors to meet their needs—and generally already have one.[12]

---

11. Ibid.
12. Ibid.

45

Poker players are value buyers who have learned that they can get high value at a low price.[13]

---

13. Ibid.

Section II: Pricing Strategies

46

It's unlikely that price buyers will be among your most profitable customers, but, with the right pricing strategy, any other kind can be.

47

Focusing on service values (like downtime costs + proper communications) can yield strong, profitable customer relationships.

48

A "good/better/best" pricing model is often a very effective strategy for segmenting both customers and products/services.

49

The "good/better/best" model requires that customers give up something to get a lower price.

Section III: Pricing New Products and Services

Section III
Pricing New Products and Services

In our competitive world one corporate mantra has become "grow or die." While growth can be achieved through acquisition, a balance of acquisition and organic growth can often provide optimum results and a very positive view of the company as an innovator by investors and customers alike. New product development is usually the lifeblood of organic growth. It can also be a very expensive and risky endeavor. Integrating strategic pricing into the new-product development process can help reduce the risks by helping to ensure that the product can provide the desired sales revenues and return on investment.

In the 1970s and 1980s companies began abandoning the old "lob it over the wall" method of product development, where engineers conceived and designed a product, then handed it over to the production team for manufacturing. It was replaced by the "stage gate" development process that focused on up-front planning and interdepartmental teams. It has been a game changer for new products. Before stage gate, new products were expected to have flaws that would get worked out as production progressed. When you bought a new car, for example, you weren't surprised if it had a few things wrong. Today, we expect a product to be perfect from the get-go, and they usually are thanks to stage gate product development.

As competition has intensified it has also become more critical to get the pricing right from the start since pricing the product either too high or too low at launch may also have lasting effects on its success in the marketplace. Integrating strategic pricing early in the process is another game changer that either helps ensure the success of the product or confirms a decision to kill it before a large amount of time and money have been spent on development.

Section III: Pricing New Products and Services

Pricing is just as important a part of new services as it is new physical products. The ability for a new service to grow, attract customers, hold off competition, or improve margins, depends upon implementing the proper pricing strategy for the launch of the service.

In this section, we will take a look at key aspects of both new-product and new-service pricing and the potential pitfalls of not doing them well.

50

Pricing new offerings presents demanding challenges in marketing, whether for revolutionary, evolutionary, or follower products.[14]

---

[14] "Pricing New Products and Innovations Effectively," *The Journal of Professional Pricing* (2009).

Section III: Pricing New Products and Services

51

Pricing development for a new product should begin by the time the product concept, attributes, and advantages are clearly articulated.

52

The pricing of products based on "benefits" versus "value" frequently leads to both overpricing and underpricing.

53

Obtaining the "voice of the customer" early in the development is a critical element of new-product pricing.

54

Involving important potential customers early in the development process often helps to jump start early sales of a new product.

Section III: Pricing New Products and Services

55

Pricing strategy for a product improvement will be very different from that of a new-to-world product.

___

___

___

56

There is a range of new product development types to consider: improvements, line extensions, complements, new-to-market, and new-to-world.

___

___

___

57

Even for a product improvement, pricing opportunities may be lost by merely extrapolating the price based on existing products.

58

Pricing strategy for a new product should include strategies to address potential competitive reactions to the product.

Section III: Pricing New Products and Services

59

Developing long-range price forecasts for new products helps to determine their true ROI and potential timing for upgrades or replacements.

60

The strategic rationale for new-service pricing is often more complex than the pricing of physical products.

61

Price should help address new-service concerns, including speed and depth of market penetration, customer retention, and margin protection.

62

Compared to new-product pricing, the intangible and inelastic nature of services provides more opportunities for new-service pricing.

63

Intangibility of services allows for various charging unit options (e.g., flat rate, variable usage, usage by user/asset & share of value).

64

A combination of a fixed minimum charge plus a usage charge can be a viable strategy.

65

It is important to analyze and understand your fixed and variable costs as a sanity check before setting fixed and variable usage charges.

_____

_____

_____

66

Inelasticity makes a competition-based new service strategy potentially viable, but only as it relates to the market leader.

_____

_____

_____

Section III: Pricing New Products and Services

67

A key step in developing a new service is to assess the market leader's service offering and pricing strategy.

68

Earned discounts based on service economies of scale may be employed to incent the customer to use the service more frequently.

69

New-service pricing strategies to avoid include: price by the hour, market-based pricing, and negotiated discounts.

Section IV: Strategic Pricing Goals and Metrics

Section IV
Strategic Pricing Goals and Metrics

As with any process improvement endeavor, it is important to establish metrics, or Key Performance Indicators (KPIs), that allow you to measure progress against your goals. There should be two sets of metrics. A set of high-level metrics should be developed for regular executive reporting and review, and also included in the overall company performance plan. These KPIs should cover each of the key internal functional areas of your business that impact the success of your strategic pricing strategies. An additional set of detail metrics are required for analysis by the pricing team to drill down to the product and customer levels, ferret out opportunities, and improve profitability. Examples of detail metrics include gross margin and net margin by product line, part number, and customer.

The chart below (Figure 2) illustrates an example set of high-level metrics.

Strategic Pricing Key Process Indicators				
Functional Area	Metric	2012 Actual	2013 Plan	YTD
Pricing, Marketing, Sales	Same Part Avg. YOY Price Increase (%)	0.80%	2%	1.30%
Pricing, Marketing, Purchasing, Operations	% Cost Increase Recovery	54%	100%	70%
	% Line Items with GM < 15%	20%	10%	16%
	Average Quote Speed (hours)	9.5	<8	10
	Quote Win Rate %	30%	40%	34%
Pricing, Marketing	Total List Price Increase ($)	$100k	$200k	$120k
Pricing, Marketing, Sales	Total OEM Price Increase ($)	$80k	$150k	$70k
Pricing, Marketing	Competitive Price Alignment (%)	60%	90%	75%
Pricing, Marketing, Engineering	Strategic Pricing Integration in New Product Projects (%)	50%	100%	80%

Figure 2

70

"What gets measured gets attention.
What gets attention gets done."
- Dr. W. Edwards Deming

_____

_____

_____

71

KPIs should be consistent with overall business objectives and include financial, process improvement, and customer service objectives.

72

Specific KPIs should be used as personal performance measures for senior management and functional areas that impact pricing.

Section IV: Strategic Pricing Goals and Metrics

73

Accurate data collection and validation is often one of the most challenging parts of strategic pricing implementation.

_____
_____
_____

74

Much of the data is typically "mined" from a company's existing information systems by pricing, finance, sales, and marketing.

75

Pricing analysis converts the data from multiple parts of the business into information useful for measuring pricing process effectiveness.

Section IV: Strategic Pricing Goals and Metrics

76

Once the KPIs have been selected, IT is often called upon to help create routines to facilitate monthly data collection and validation.

77

A pricing team will collect, analyze, and report the KPI data to senior management.

78

A monthly status and progress review of the high-level KPIs should be conducted by senior management with the pricing team.

Section IV: Strategic Pricing Goals and Metrics

79

For metrics that are not on track to achieve annual goals, corrective actions must be developed and discussed during the monthly review.

80

Preparations for monthly reviews drives the detail processes that are geared towards continuous improvement of the overall pricing process.

81

Price-detail reports facilitate the setting of optimum pricing for product lines or individual products consistent with KPI objectives.

82

Price-detail reports clearly identify low-margin product lines, products, and customers, providing focus for improvement actions.

Section IV: Strategic Pricing Goals and Metrics

83

Win-rate and quoting speed reports help validate pricing levels and identify opportunities to improve customer satisfaction and sales.

_____

_____

_____

84

Competitive price alignment does not mean pricing the same as competitors. Alignment includes premiums for increased product value.

85

When diligently practiced, metrics development & tracking/reviewing them becomes a significant profit driver & continuous-improvement tool.

Section V: Implementing a Strategic Pricing Process for Your Business

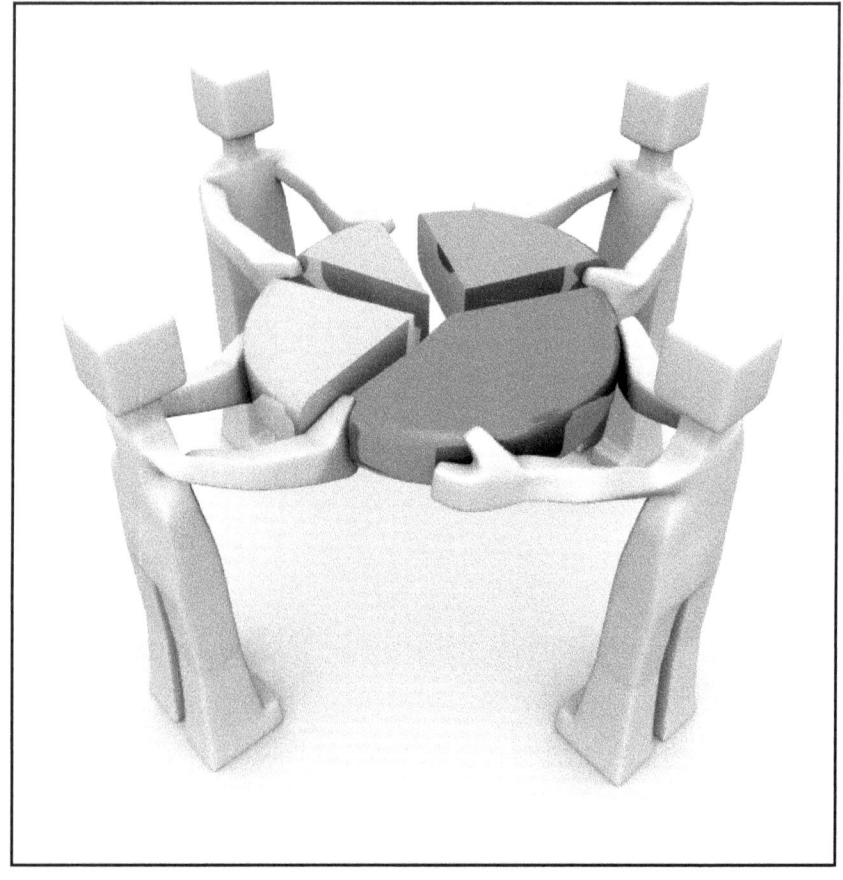

Section V
Implementing a Strategic Pricing Process for Your Business

In order to effectively implement and coordinate the key activities outlined in Sections I through IV, an overall pricing process must be developed and the key players in the process must be organized and empowered to make it happen. The pricing process is most successful when it is driven from the top down. That is not to say that it is managed from the top, but key pricing management personnel must have an executive "charter" to enforce the process. A key element in the pricing process is a pricing team to manage and enforce the process. The process must be documented and include such items as: specific pricing authority levels, a quoting process, new-product pricing, and regular pricing reports driven by a set of analytics to track ongoing progress towards achieving the pricing KPIs. It is essential to have a pricing leader to manage the function. The pricing leader is often part of a matrix organization and is supported by team members from functions such as marketing, accounting, and customer service. Larger firms may have an integrated pricing team that includes pricers and data analysts.

The chart on the next page (Figure 3) illustrates an example of a pricing authority matrix used as a guide for management and the pricing team.

Section V: Implementing a Strategic Pricing Process for Your Business

Pricing Approval Limits					
Authority	List Prices	Discounts	Promotions	New Products	Special Projects
Pricing Manager	no	15% maximum	no	<$50k forecasted annual sales	OK within standard margin levels and <$100k in sales
Sales and Marketing Mgr	May increase but not decrease	20% maximum	Up to $50k cost of promotion	Up to $100k forecasted annual sales	OK within standard margin levels and up to $200k in sales
Vice President	May increase or decrease	30% maximum and up to $200k sales	>$50k to $200k cost of promotion	>$100k and up to $500k in forecasted annual sales	Up to $500k in sales and/or special margin levels
President	Must approve decreases with >$200k impact	>30% discount and over $200k in sales	$>200k cost of promotion	$>500k forecasted annual sales	All projects >$500k and special margin levels

Figure 3

86

When companies focus on pricing and get disparate units to operate in sync, they typically deliver at least a 3-point improvement in EBIT.[15]

87

For a company with $50 million of annual sales, a good strategic pricing process can add up to $1.5 million to the bottom line.

---

15. George Stalk, Jr, "Organizing for Pricing," *The Journal of Professional Pricing*, 2003.

88

Employing a full-time pricing leader to implement and manage the process (assisted by a cross-functional team) yields an impressive ROI.

89

The optimal candidate for a pricing leader is often a current company employee with good analytical skills and product knowledge.

90

The pricing leader must be able to effectively gain the cooperation of cross-functional team members.

91

The pricing organization can be centralized, decentralized, or center-led, depending upon the size and structure of the firm.

92

A center-led pricing organization allows core pricing fundamentals to be consistent throughout the organization as it grows.

_____
_____
_____

93

A center-led organization allows recognition for specific pricing strategies that may differ among product lines, customers, and markets.

_____
_____
_____

94

To succeed, the pricing team must have the support of senior management, regardless of the type of pricing organization selected.

95

A key role of senior management is to ensure that pricing goals and KPIs are aligned with overall company goals.

96

Senior management must be instrumental in the establishment and enforcement of pricing authority limits.

97

Senior management's monthly review of pricing KPI progress with the pricing team can usually be done in 30 minutes; it is time well spent.

98

A detailed price assessment that can identify specific opportunities within the pricing segments is critical to an effective program.[16]

_____

16. Bernstein, "Managing Limited Resources to Improve Profitability."

99

A detailed price assessment is an important precursor to the development of the pricing process and KPIs for your company.

100

Sets of pricing analytics can be used to support pricing assessments and the development of ongoing pricing analyses and reports.

Section V: Implementing a Strategic Pricing Process for Your Business

101

Pricing analytical tools include price waterfall charts, price scatter plots, and a variety of reports generated from accounting data.[17]

---

17. Examples of key pricing analytics are provided in the appendix.

102

The results of a price assessment will reveal product or service areas that should be prioritized for pricing action.

103

Items with excessive "price leakage" are a good starting point for action as opportunities are frequently the most abundant there.

104

Price leakage is often a transactional issue and is illustrated most clearly by a price waterfall.[18]

_____

_____

_____

---

18. See the section on price waterfalls in the appendix.

105

Early integration of strategic pricing into new-product development helps prevent past pricing mistakes from creeping into new products.

106

A set of consistent guidelines to optimize pricing can often cover 80% or more of total sales transactions.

Section V: Implementing a Strategic Pricing Process for Your Business

107

When both inside and field sales are trained on price guidelines, quote turnaround time and customer satisfaction are typically improved.

___

108

Large and/or complex quotes not covered by pricing guidelines can be handled in a timely manner by pricing specialists and managers.

109

It is often helpful to develop a pricing calendar that describes daily, weekly, monthly, and annual activities for the pricing team.

Section VI: Implementing Price Changes

Section VI
Implementing Price Changes

Sales and marketing people hate to ask customers for price increases. They expect a negative reaction and often get one. Careful planning by the strategic pricing leader (with cooperation from sales and marketing) can help reduce the stress and the negative effects of communicating price increases. The pricing leader can accomplish this heady task by analyzing all parts, customers, and markets[19] to select the right parts, the right customers, and the right price level increases. Planning for a price change should typically start three to four months prior to execution so that the proper sales and marketing inputs, profit improvement estimates, and management approvals can be obtained. In addition, advanced notice and explanation is provided to the sales force, and then to the customer. Well planned and executed price changes can actually increase customer satisfaction and the credibility of the seller. Review the sample price change plan on the next page as an example (Figure 4).

---

19. See appendix.

Section VI: Implementing Price Changes

	Price Change Plan for July 1, 2013		Timeline							
Item	Description	Resp.	15-Mar	31-Mar	15-Apr	30-Apr	15-May	31-May	15-Jun	1-Jul
1	Define Overall Price Change Target (%)	SrM	▲							
2	Review Low margin accounts for opportunities	PL	▲							
3	Review Low margin product lines and part numbers for opportunities	PL	▲							
4	Conduct/ update competitive alignment analysis	PL/MM		▲						
5	Obtain special customer opportunity inputs from Sales & Marketing	PL/MM /SM		▲						
6	Obtain potential product cost changes from Operations and Procurement	PL			▲					
7	Model price change scenario based on data collected & compare to target	PL				▲				
8	Review results and revisit opportunities as required to achieve target	PL/MM /SM				▲				
9	Review price change proposal key elements with senior management / adjust / obtain approval	PL/MM /SM					▲			
10	Develop internal and external communications for price change.	PL/MM /SM						▲		
11	Review communications proposal with mgmt and obtain approval	PL/MM /SM					▲			
12	Communicate price change rationale and details to internal/ sales staff	PL/MM /SM						▲		
13	Communicate price change rationale and details to direct customers	SM/SS							▲	
14	Communicate price change rationale and details to distribution	PL/MM							▲	
15	Develop and test price change input files for business system	PL/IT								▲
16	Implement price changes in business system effective for all new orders	IT								▲

PL= Pricing Leader
SrM= Senior Management
MM= Marketing Manager

SM= Sales Manager
SS= Sales Staff
IT= Information Technology

Figure 4[20]

---

20. To see a larger version of this chart, please visit http://bit.ly/b2b_figure4.

110

"Customer reaction and resistance to a price increase is directly related to its impact on their business."[21]

111

Plan a price increase carefully. Examine the data and understand the customer's potential substitution situation for the product.

---

21. Brian Wanless, "Raising Prices and Making It Stick," *The Journal of Professional Pricing* (December 2004).

Section VI: Implementing Price Changes

112

Price increases can come in many forms, including surcharges, reduction of discounts, delaying price reductions, and shorter payment terms.

113

Surcharges and delaying price reductions are temporary measures utilized for situations that impact short-term costs or capacity.

114

Effectively increase prices by eliminating lower-priced products and increasing focus on customers that are willing to pay more.

115

Include all potential forms of price increase in your price-increase-plan check list, even if they will not be utilized.

Section VI: Implementing Price Changes

116

Key elements of making a price change include customer, competitor, and margin analysis, and effective communication of the price change.

117

The key analysis and communication elements for making a price change are equally important for either increases or decreases in pricing.

_____
_____
_____

Section VI: Implementing Price Changes

118

Customers must be effectively segmented by both market and whether they are serviced directly or through distribution.

119

Customer segmentation affects both the type of price change that should be utilized and the communications thereof.

120

When considering a price reduction, do the math before taking action.

121

A 5% price reduction on a 35% gross margin item will require a 16.7% increase in volume to achieve the same gross profit dollars.

Section VI: Implementing Price Changes

122

Price communications should be designed to minimize the likelihood that customers or competitors will misread your pricing rationale.[22]

_____
22. Johnson, "How to Organize the Pricing Discipline."

123

Having your own prices misread by competitors can be just as damaging as you misreading theirs; both can start a price war.[23]

124

Provide your sales force with advanced notice of a price increase and a clear explanation that they can communicate to their customers.

---

23. Ibid.

Section VI: Implementing Price Changes

125

A salesperson should be able to meet with their customer, explain a price change, and confidently defend the value provided by your firm.

126

A personal visit may not be practical for communicating price changes to all distributors or agents, but the message is the same: value.

127

To respect their needs for planning, communicate a price change to customers and distribution 30 to 60 days before implementation.

Section VII: Continuous Improvement

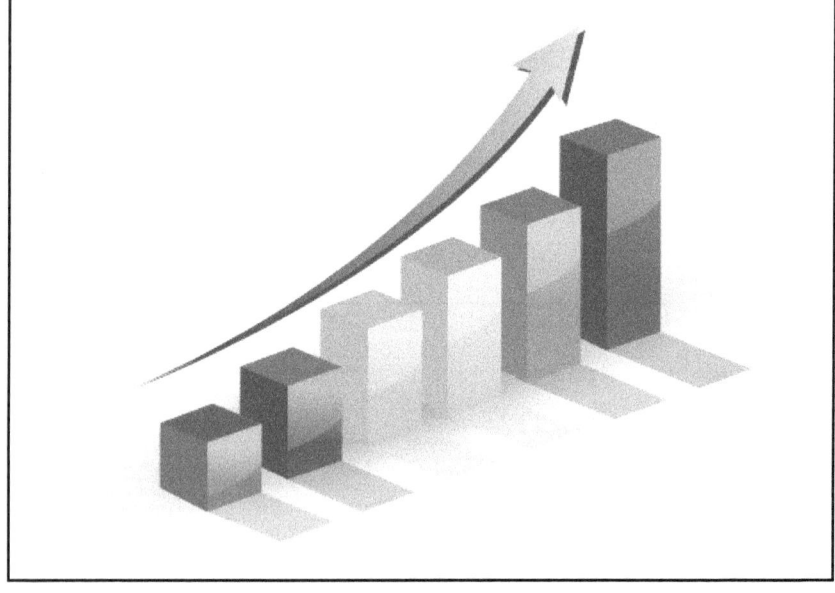

Section VII
Continuous Improvement

In this section, we will wrap up our discussion of strategic pricing process development with a look at key actions required for continuous process improvement. Continuous improvement is required for all business processes if you want to achieve long-term profitable growth—strategic pricing is no exception. Process improvement should be built in since pricing is such a dynamic variable that is influenced by costs, competition, and customer needs. If you implement strategic pricing with the key elements that have been presented in the first six sections, the process is already primed for continuous improvement. After all, if you're regularly (at least annually) reassessing your competitive alignment, market and customer opportunities, changes in costs, development of new products, along with the monthly monitoring of your KPIs, you are already looking at most of the elements that are the keys to continuous improvement.

Section VII: Continuous Improvement

128

Think of the development of the strategic-pricing process as a journey rather than a once-and-done implementation.

_____
_____
_____

129

Achieving pricing excellence will typically take a few years, even for well-executed implementations.

130

Integrate continuous improvement into your pricing function just as you would for other key business functions in your firm.

Section VII: Continuous Improvement

131

Ongoing training and development of your pricing leader in new methods and techniques should be a core part of continuous improvement.

_____

_____

_____

132

The Professional Pricing Society™ (PricingSociety.com) is an excellent resource for ongoing training of pricing leaders.

_____

_____

_____

133

Based on the results of monthly KPI reviews, make adjustments to your pricing process on a regular basis as needed.

_____
_____
_____

Section VII: Continuous Improvement

134

Raise the bar on KPIs annually and/or add new ones based on the progress achieved throughout the year and new issues that may arise.

135

Implement a win/loss database for reference by the pricing team when developing new quotes.

136

Analyze win/loss data to understand the key contributors to losses <u>and</u> to wins. Price and non-price factors should be considered.

137

Conduct customer research in key market segments to fully understand what they most value from your products and services.

Section VII: Continuous Improvement

138

Consider investing in pricing software to optimize both your price setting and quote speed, while building an effective pricing database.

139

A benefit of pricing software: the consolidation of pricing analytics into one integrated program (replacing homegrown analytics).

140

A well-deployed and practiced pricing process will surely result in pricing excellence and higher profits.

What Are Your Ahas?

Thank you for reading *#B2B STRATEGIC PRICING tweet*!
Got any "ahas" that would fit with this book?

We'd love for you to share them!

Tweet us **@thinkaha** and tag your ahas with **#b2bstrategicpricing** or **#b2bpricing** (depending on your character count).

Appendix: Pricing Analytics

This appendix contains examples of analytical tools utilized in strategic pricing. The data utilized to create these tools is typically located in a company's financial, ERP, or CRM systems. These tools and others allow the firm to effectively pursue pricing improvements as well as measure and track the KPIs described in Section IV.

The Price Waterfall Chart

The price waterfall chart is an extremely useful tool in identifying price leakage and providing guidance on where to attack this common problem. Price leakage is the accumulation of sales transaction elements that reduce the effective price of the product or service. The sample price waterfall chart shown on the next page (Figure 5) breaks down the amount of sales revenue that is lost in the overall sales transaction process. The final price actually received is often called the "pocket price" and is often far less than the reported sales revenue. Use this chart to segregate the various price-reducing elements and identify the areas of opportunity to improve the pocket price. It makes the task of reducing price leakage easier by taking small, focused actions in a few select areas to regain some of that lost revenue.

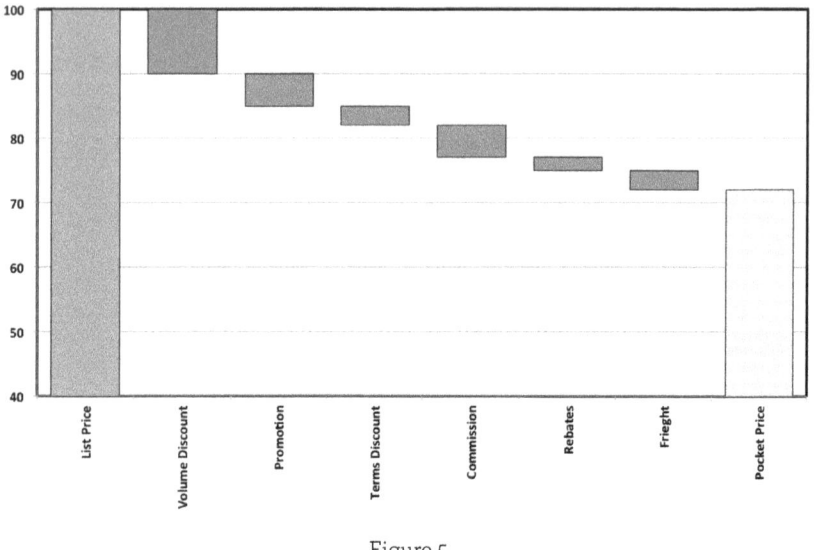

Figure 5

Price Dispersion Chart

The price dispersion chart is a tool used to assess the state of price discounts versus volume in the company. It is designed to determine whether the currently practiced price/volume logic is sound. The expectation is that high-volume customers should receive greater discounts than low-volume customers. It is not unusual for the price data to yield a chart (as shown in Figure 6) where a cluster of low-volume accounts are getting disproportionately large discounts. There are several reasons why this happens, including promises by customers of higher sales volume that haven't materialized. Pricing at these accounts should be reviewed for adjustment to more rational levels.

This dispersion chart, typical of most companies, indicates that the pricing policies are discouraging the sample company from strategically managing discounting. Instead, the customers—who are the best negotiators—are getting the best prices.

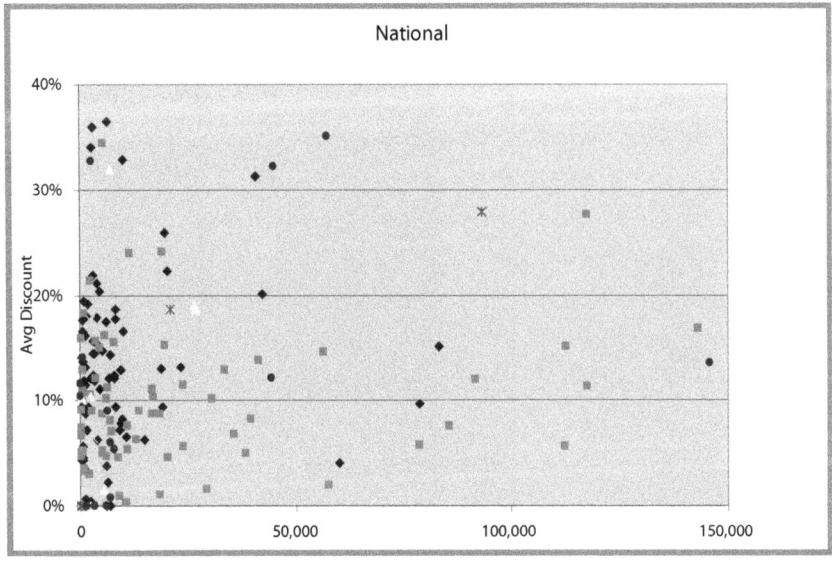

Figure 6[24]

Reports

A few selected monthly reports extracted from internal system data can make the monthly tracking of KPIs a very manageable process. Gross margin and sales reports by customer, product line, sales channel, or sales region can provide a wealth of information—easily sorted in Microsoft Excel—to support the monthly tracking of KPIs. There are also several integrated pricing software programs which can automate the monthly tracking function. Utilization of an integrated pricing program should be seriously considered as a long-term solution to data collection, analysis, and reporting. Sales can also use some programs in the field as a tool to provide rapid response to customer quote requests.

---

24. Paul Hunt, "Capturing a Fair Return for the Value Delivered," *The Pricing Advisor*, August 2006, http://members.pricingsociety.com/articles/PPS-06-Aug-newsletter-Article-3.pdf.

About the Author

Bob Bonacorsi is the founder of ProfitSmart Solutions, LLC, an independent strategic pricing and marketing consulting firm.

ProfitSmart Solutions, LLC helps companies create an ongoing, sustainable path to sales growth and increased profit margins. Bob provides strategic pricing, market, product, and competitive analysis services to clients in manufacturing and service industries.

Having held key leadership positions for more than twenty years, Bob has an astute understanding of marketing, product development, operations management, and business processes.

Bob holds a Bachelor of Science in mechanical engineering from Purdue University and a Master of Business Administration from Kent State University. He has also achieved the Certified Pricing Professional (CPP) designation from the Professional Pricing Society.

Books in the THiNKaha® Series

The THiNKaha book series is for thinking adults who lack the time or desire to read long books, but want to improve themselves with knowledge of the most up-to-date subjects. THiNKaha is a leader in timely, cutting-edge books and mobile applications from relevant experts that provide valuable information in a fun, Twitter-brief format for a fast-paced world.

They are available online at http://thinkaha.com or at other online and physical bookstores.

1. #AFTER COLLEGE tweet by Matthew Chow and Jonathan Chu
2. #B2B STRATEGIC PRICING tweet by Bob Bonacorsi, CPP
3. #BOOK TITLE tweet by Roger C. Parker
4. #BUSINESS SAVVY PM tweet by Cinda Voegtli
5. #COACHING tweet by Sterling Lanier
6. Coffee Crazy by Robert Galinsky
7. #CONTENT MARKETING tweet by Ambal Balakrishnan
8. #CORPORATE CULTURE tweet by S. Chris Edmonds
9. #CORPORATE GOVERNANCE tweet by Brad Beckstead, CPA, CISA, CRISC
10. #CREATING THOUGHT LEADERS tweet by Mitchell Levy
11. #CROWDSOURCING tweet by Kiruba Shankar and Mitchell Levy
12. #CULTURAL TRANSFORMATION tweet by Melissa Lamson
13. #DEATHtweet Book01: A Well-Lived Life through 140 Perspectives on Death and Its Teachings by Timothy Tosta
14. #DEATH tweet Book02: 140 Perspectives on Being a Supportive Witness to the End of Life by Timothy Tosta
15. #DEMAND GENERATION tweet by Gaurav Kumar
16. #DIVERSITYtweet by Deepika Bajaj
17. #DOG tweet by Timothy Tosta and Nancy Martin
18. #DREAMtweet by Joe Heuer
19. #ENDURANCE tweet by Jarie Bolander
20. #ENGAGE tweet by Maryann Baumgarten, PhD, and Lisa Smith
21. #ENTRYLEVELtweet Book01: Taking Your Career from Classroom to Cubicle by Heather R. Huhman
22. #ENTRY LEVEL tweet Book02: Relevant Advice for Students and New Graduates in the Day of Social Media by Christine Ruff and Lori Ruff

23. *#EXPERT EXCEL PROJECTS tweet* by Larry Moseley
24. *#GOOGLE+ for BUSINESS tweet* by Janet Fouts
25. *#GREAT BOSSES tweet* by S. Chris Edmonds, MHROD
26. *#HEALTHCARE REFORM tweet* by Jason T. Andrew
27. *#IT OPERATIONS MANAGEMENT tweet* by Peter Spielvogel, Jon Haworth, Sonja Hickey
28. *#JOBSEARCHtweet* by Barbara Safani
29. *#LEADERSHIPtweet* by Kevin Eikenberry
30. *#LEADS to SALES tweet* by Jim McAvoy
31. *#LEAN SIX SIGMA tweet* by Dr. Shree R. Nanguneri
32. *#LEAN STARTUP tweet* by Seymour Duncker
33. *#MANAGING UP tweet* by Tony Deblauwe and Patrick Reilly
34. *#MANAGING YOUR VIRTUAL BOSS tweet* by Carmela Southers
35. *#MILLENNIALtweet* by Alexandra Levit
36. *#MOJOtweet* by Marshall Goldsmith
37. *#MOVING OUT tweet* by Gabrielle Jasinski, Eliza Lamson, Elizabeth Wassmann, and Hannah Miller
38. *#MY BRAND tweet* by Laura Lowell
39. *#OPEN TEXTBOOK tweet* by Sharyn Fitzpatrick
40. *#PARTNER tweet* by Chaitra Vedullapalli
41. *#PLAN to WIN tweet* by Ron Snyder and Eric Doner
42. *#POSITIVITY at WORK tweet* by S. Chris Edmonds, MHROD and Lisa Zigarmi, MAPP
43. *#POWER KIDS tweet* by Rudy Mui and Shirley Woo
44. *#PRESENTATION tweet* by Wayne Turmel
45. *#PRIVACY tweet* by Lori Ruff
46. *#PROJECT MANAGEMENT tweet* by Guy Ralfe and Himanshu Jhamb
47. *#QUALITYtweet* by Tanmay Vora
48. *#RISK MANAGEMENT tweet* by Cinda Voegtli & Laura Erkeneff
49. *#SCRAPPY GENERAL MANAGEMENT tweet* by Michael Horton
50. *#SCRUM tweet* by Utpal Vaishnav
51. *#SKATEBOARDING tweet* by Tad Malone
52. *#SOCIAL MEDIA PR tweet* by Janet Fouts
53. *#SOCIALMEDIA NONPROFIT tweet* by Janet Fouts with Beth Kanter
54. *#SPORTS tweet* by Ronnie Lott with Keith Potter

55. *#STANDARDS tweet* by Karen Bartleson
56. *#STUDENT SUCCESS tweet* by Marie B. Highby and Julia C. Schmitt
57. *#SUCCESSFUL CORPORATE LEARNING tweet Book01: Profitable Training by Optimizing your Customer and Partner Education Organization* by Terry Lydon and Mitchell Levy
58. *#SUCCESSFUL CORPORATE LEARNING tweet Book02: Critical Skills All Learning Professionals Can Put to Use Today* by Bill Cushard and Mitchell Levy
59. *#SUCCESSFUL CORPORATE LEARNING tweet Book03: Instructional Design for Today's Professionals* by Vicki Halsey, S. Chris Edmonds, and Mitchell Levy
60. *#SUCCESSFUL CORPORATE LEARNING tweet Book04: Career Transition Training and Services That Work in Today's Environment* by Barbara Safani and Mitchell Levy
61. *#SUCCESSFUL CORPORATE LEARNING tweet Book05: Everything You Need to Know about Knowledge Management in Practice in 140 Characters or Less* by Michael Prevou and Mitchell Levy
62. *#SUCCESSFUL CORPORATE LEARNING tweet Book06: Creating a Learning Culture with 140 Specific Ideas for Building Continual Learning into Organizational Life* by Kevin Eikenberry and Mitchell Levy
63. *#SUCCESSFUL CORPORATE LEARNING tweet Book07: Everything You Need to Know about Communities of Practice* by Mike Hower, Michael Prevou, and Mitchell Levy
64. *#SUCCESSFUL CORPORATE LEARNING tweet Book08: 140 Tips and Tricks for Creating and Delivering Powerful, High-Quality Webinars, and Virtual Learning Events* by Sharyn Fitzpatrick and Mitchell Levy
65. *#SUCCESSFUL CORPORATE LEARNING tweet Book09: Collaborative Tools and Techniques to Empower Productivity and Learning* by David Coleman and Mitchell Levy
66. *#SUCCESSFUL CORPORATE LEARNING tweet Book10: Making Learning Stick—Transforming Knowledge into Performance* by John Moxley, PhD, and Mitchell Levy
67. *#TEAMWORK tweet* by Caroline G. Nicholl
68. *#THINKtweet* by Rajesh Setty
69. *#THOUGHT LEADERSHIP tweet* by Liz Alexander, PhD and Craig Badings
70. *#TOXINS tweet* by Laurel J. Standley, PhD
71. *The Unofficial Harry Potter Spell Book* by Duncan Levy

www.ingramcontent.com/pod-product-compliance
Ingram Content Group UK Ltd.
Pitfield, Milton Keynes, MK11 3LW, UK
UKHW021303180426
11947UKWH00015B/992